under the ocean
explore & discover
the seas around New Zealand

by Gillian Candler
illustrated by Ned Barraud

craig potton publishing

For my mum, Jenny — NB
For Olaf — GC

Ned Barraud is an illustrator with a keen passion for the natural world. When not illustrating, he works on films at Weta Digital as a texture artist. He often visits the beaches around the wild Wellington coastline where you can spot many of the creatures found in this book.

Gillian Candler has been a teacher and worked in educational publishing for many years. She now works as a writer and consultant. She enjoys looking at the sea from her writing desk, watching flocks of seabirds, and keeping an eye out for dolphins and whales.

First published in 2014 by Craig Potton Publishing

Craig Potton Publishing
98 Vickerman Street, PO Box 555, Nelson,
New Zealand
www.craigpotton.co.nz

Text © Gillian Candler; illustrations © Ned Barraud

ISBN PB 978-1-927213-08-7; HB 978-1-927213-09-4

Printed in China by Midas Printing International Ltd

This book is copyright. Apart from any fair dealing for the purposes of private study, research, criticism or review, as permitted under the Copyright Act, no part may be reproduced by any process without the permission of the publishers.

 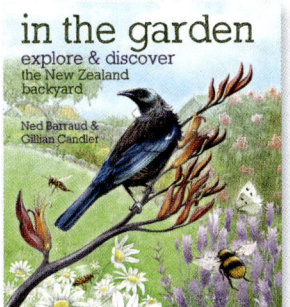

Also by Ned Barraud and Gillian Candler
At the Beach: Explore and discover the New Zealand seashore and *In the Garden: Explore and discover the New Zealand backyard.*

contents

The ocean   4
Reefs & the sea floor   6
What lives in the reefs?   8
What lives on the sea floor?   10
Open ocean   12
What lives out in the open ocean?   14
The deep, deep ocean   16
Animals of land & sea   18
Plankton & other small sea creatures   20
Squid, octopuses, crayfish & crabs   22
Rays & sharks   24
More fish   26
Whales   28
Dolphins   30
Seals & penguins   32
Seabirds   34
Glossary, index & find out more   36

All around our islands, as far as the eye can see, is ocean.

Calm and blue one day, stormy and grey the next, the seas around New Zealand are full of life.

From the land we see only a few of the animals that live under the ocean. Sometimes dolphins leap out of the water or a whale comes up for air. Diving seabirds show us where fish and squid are swimming just below the surface. But most creatures never come near the surface of the ocean. They live on the sea floor, hiding in rocky reefs or in the deep, deep ocean.

Turn the pages of this book to find out more about the hidden creatures that live in the ocean.

reefs & the sea floor

Beyond the coast, the sea floor is as varied as the land, with forests of seaweed, rocky reefs rising up like hills and valleys of smooth sand in between.

Above the sea floor, small fish keep together in large groups called schools. They dart quickly out of the way when they see danger.

Rays and sharks come visiting, looking for food.

Reefs are like cities under the sea, home to many different sea creatures. Some of the animals that live in reefs hide in rock crevices and holes. Colourful sponges and tubeworms attach themselves to the rocks.

For a closer look at what lives in and around the reefs turn to pages 8-9. For what lives on the sea floor turn to pages 10-11.

What lives in the reefs?

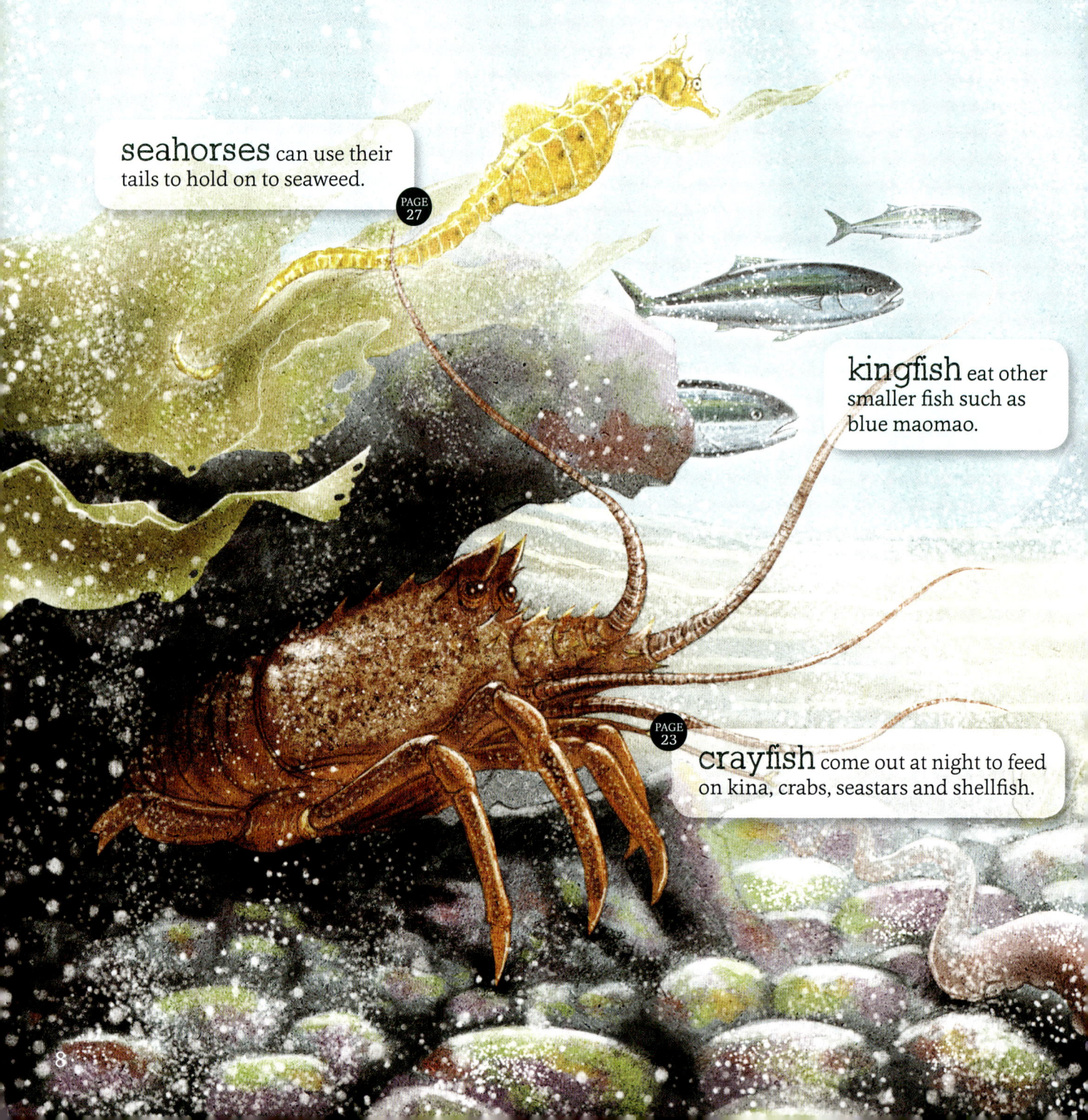

seahorses can use their tails to hold on to seaweed.

kingfish eat other smaller fish such as blue maomao.

crayfish come out at night to feed on kina, crabs, seastars and shellfish.

When in danger **porcupine fish** suck in water until they are a round, spiky ball.

PAGE 27

PAGE 21

The **clown nudibranch** is eating a sponge. It is a strange and colourful type of sea slug.

PAGE 21

tubeworms attach themselves to rocks and build a tube to live in.

PAGE 23

octopuses can camouflage themselves by changing colour and texture to match their surroundings.

What lives on the sea floor?

kelp forests provide food for animals, as well as places to hide.

This **stargazer** is hiding in the sand, ready to leap out and surprise its prey.

hiwihiwi are also called kelp fish.

This **tarakihi** is eating a brittle star.

PAGE 21

brittle stars lift their arms up to catch plankton.

PAGE 21

lace coral is made up of lots of tiny animals that live together to form a colony.

10

short-tailed rays search for animals hidden in the sand.
PAGE 24

carpet sharks feed at night time and usually hide during the day.
PAGE 24

sea cucumbers find food in the mud on the sea floor.
PAGE 21

blue cod can rest on the sea floor standing on their fins.
PAGE 26

11

open ocean

At sea, high above the sea floor, live large animals such as sharks, dolphins and whales. Some are just passing through, others stay in New Zealand's waters all year round.

The ocean currents bring together large amounts of tiny plankton, which provide food for many animals. Schools of anchovies, trevally and arrow squid feed on plankton and krill. Larger fish, such as tuna and kingfish, feed on smaller fish and in turn become food for even larger animals.

Seabirds such as sooty shearwaters dive for fish and squid.

What lives out in the open ocean?

The **mako shark** is the fastest shark in the world and can reach speeds of over 50 kilometres an hour.

PAGE 25

arrow squid are eaten by sea mammals, fish and birds.

PAGE 22

tuna migrate between the warmer waters of the Pacific Ocean and the colder waters around New Zealand, to feed and to breed.

the deep, deep ocean

Far out from land, the ocean can be thousands of metres deep. Light from the sun can't reach that far down, so animals that live here need special strategies to survive in the dark.

Some fish have large eyes that make it easier to see. Others glow, lighting up the ocean around them.

Giant squid live in the deep ocean. Sperm whales dive thousands of metres to catch them, using echolocation to find them in the dark.

animals of land & sea

Not all of the animals found in the sea can live there all year round. Some seabirds need to return to land at night. Spotted shags nest on rocky cliffs. Yellow-eyed penguins waddle across the beach to nests in the bush, after spending a day out at sea catching fish for their chicks.

Fur seals and sea lions rest on the shore. Their babies, called pups, are born on land and stay here until they are old enough to swim and find food.

19

plankton & other small sea creatures

plankton

Plankton are the most important food source in the ocean, but they are so small you need a microscope to see them. There are two main types of plankton – phytoplankton which need sunshine to grow and zooplankton which are tiny animals that eat other plankton.

krill

kōura rangi

Krill are shrimp-like creatures just a few centimetres long. Despite being so tiny they are the main food of the sea's largest animals, the baleen whales (page 29). A blue whale can eat over 3 tonnes of krill a day.

ocean food facts

- Whichever seafood you eat – fish and chips, a tuna salad or kaimoana – you can trace the source of its food right back to plankton or seaweed. The fish in your fish and chips ate smaller fish and shellfish, which in turn ate plankton or seaweed.

- Plankton float around but can't swim against the current or tides. Ocean currents and tides bring large amounts of plankton together to create good feeding areas, such as off the coast of Kaikōura where whales, seals and dolphins feed.

sea cucumber

rori

Sea cucumbers have tube feet to help them walk. They vacuum up mud and sediment from the ocean floor, filtering out the food before pooing the rest out.

brittle star

weki huna

Brittle stars usually have 5 arms which they use to crawl along the sea floor as well as to catch food. If they lose an arm, it will regrow. These brittle stars live among lace coral.

tubeworm

There are over 500 different species of tubeworm in the oceans around New Zealand. They build a tube to live in and extend their feathery tentacles out of the tube to catch plankton for food.

nudibranch

Pronounced 'noo- dee- brank', the clown nudibranch's bright colours are a warning that it is poisonous to eat. Nudibranchs are related to pāua and other shellfish, but have evolved to survive without a shell.

lace coral or bryozoans

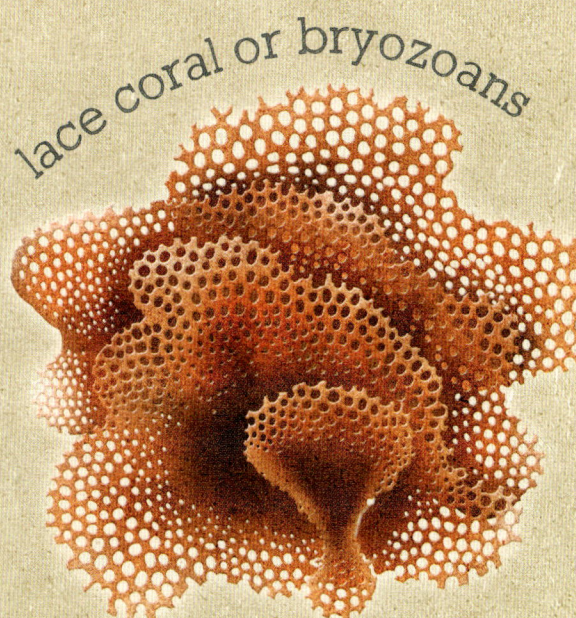

The tiny animals that make up lace coral feed on plankton. They build a structure to live in that looks like a shell or skeleton. Lace corals can't move so they rely on the ocean currents to bring food to them. There are about 950 species of lace coral around New Zealand.

squid, octopuses, crayfish & crabs

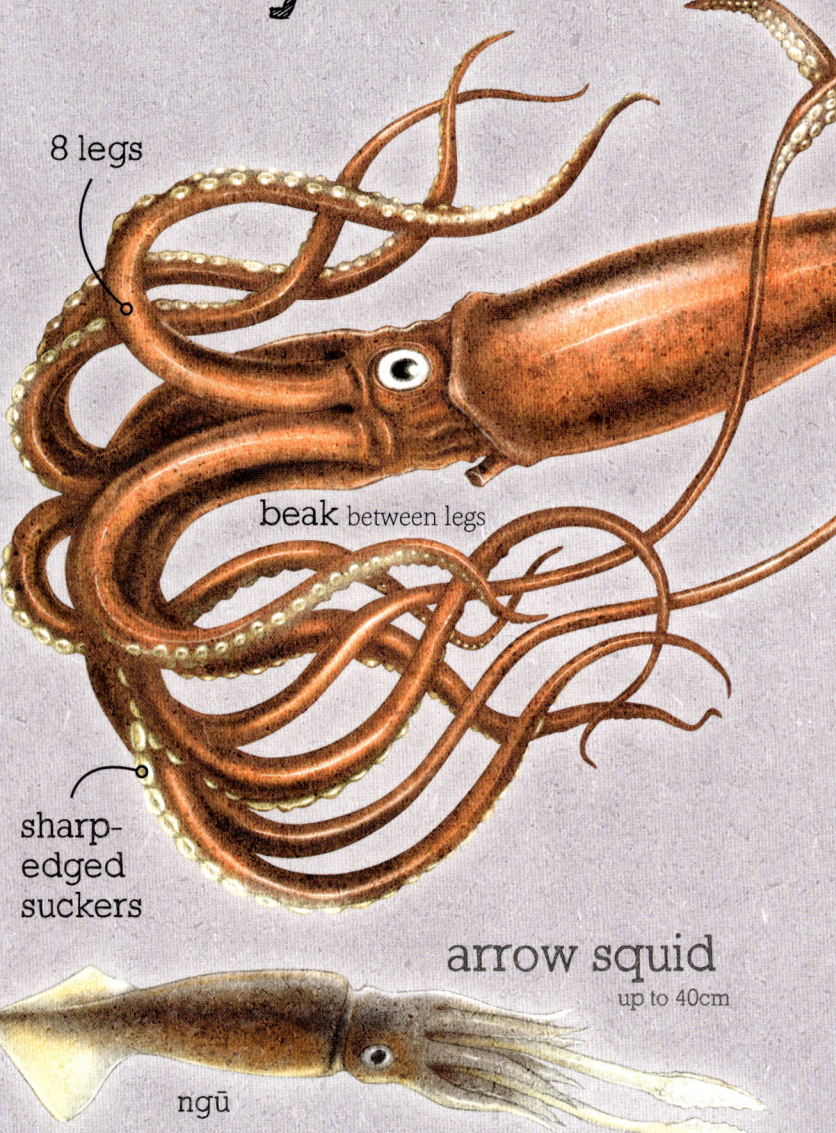

8 legs

2 tentacles

beak between legs

sharp-edged suckers

giant squid
up to 13m

Scientists who study giant squid get a lot of their information from squid that are washed up on beaches. It is thought that giant squid weigh up to 275kg. Giant squid are eaten by sperm whales – beaks of giant squid have been found in their stomachs.

arrow squid
up to 40cm

ngū

Arrow squid live in schools. They are eaten by many sea creatures including birds and whales. They are also one of the most common squid caught for people to eat.

squid facts

- Squid are predators that ambush their prey. Giant squid are thought to wait for prey to come to them, but the heavier colossal squid is more aggressive and hunts its prey.
- Squid range in size from tiny squid a few centimetres long to the giant squid and colossal squid that are both known to be up to 13m long.
- A colossal squid that is on display at Te Papa weighed 490kg when it was alive.

octopus up to 2m

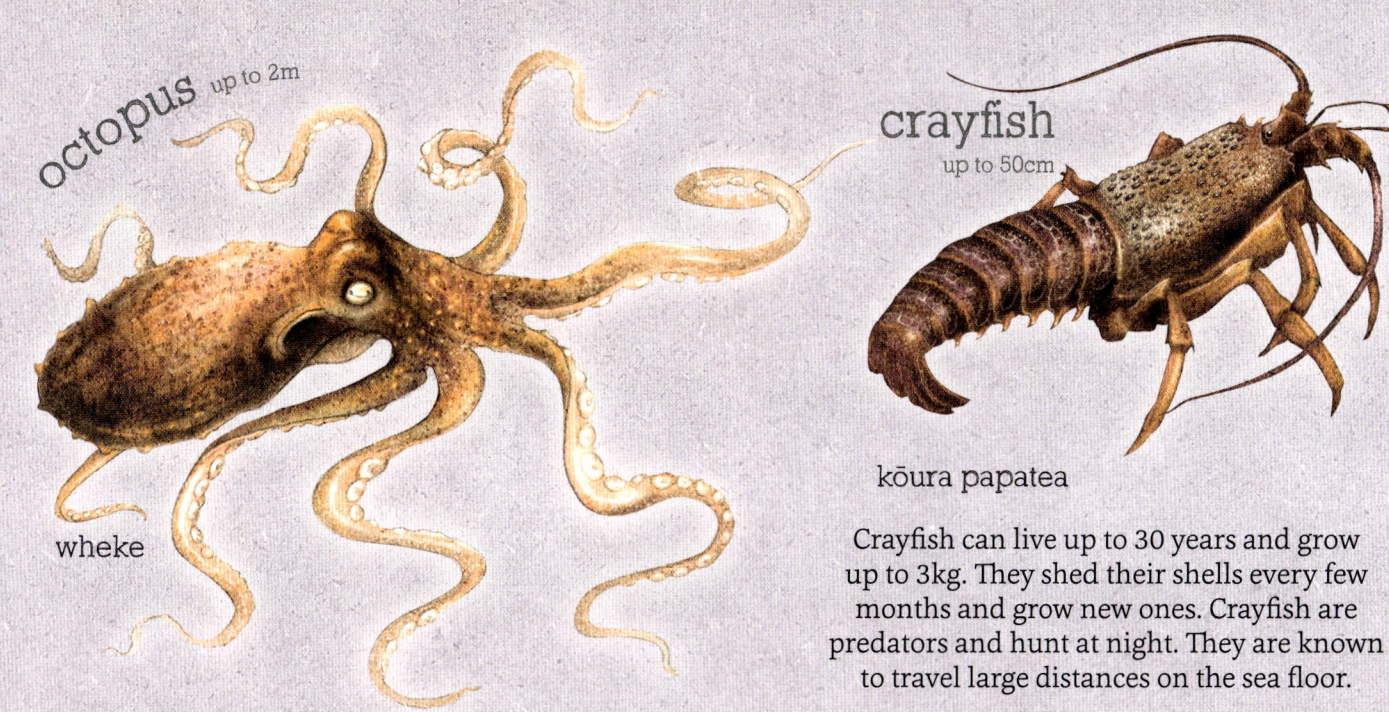

wheke

The name octopus comes from Greek and means 'eight footed'. Octopuses dig holes in the sea floor, hide in tiny spaces in reefs or build a home out of rocks. If they are threatened, octopuses can squirt out ink to distract predators. Octopuses eat shellfish and crayfish.

crayfish up to 50cm

kōura papatea

Crayfish can live up to 30 years and grow up to 3kg. They shed their shells every few months and grow new ones. Crayfish are predators and hunt at night. They are known to travel large distances on the sea floor.

king crab up to 1m

These huge crabs live deep down on the sea floor, up to 1.5km below the ocean surface.

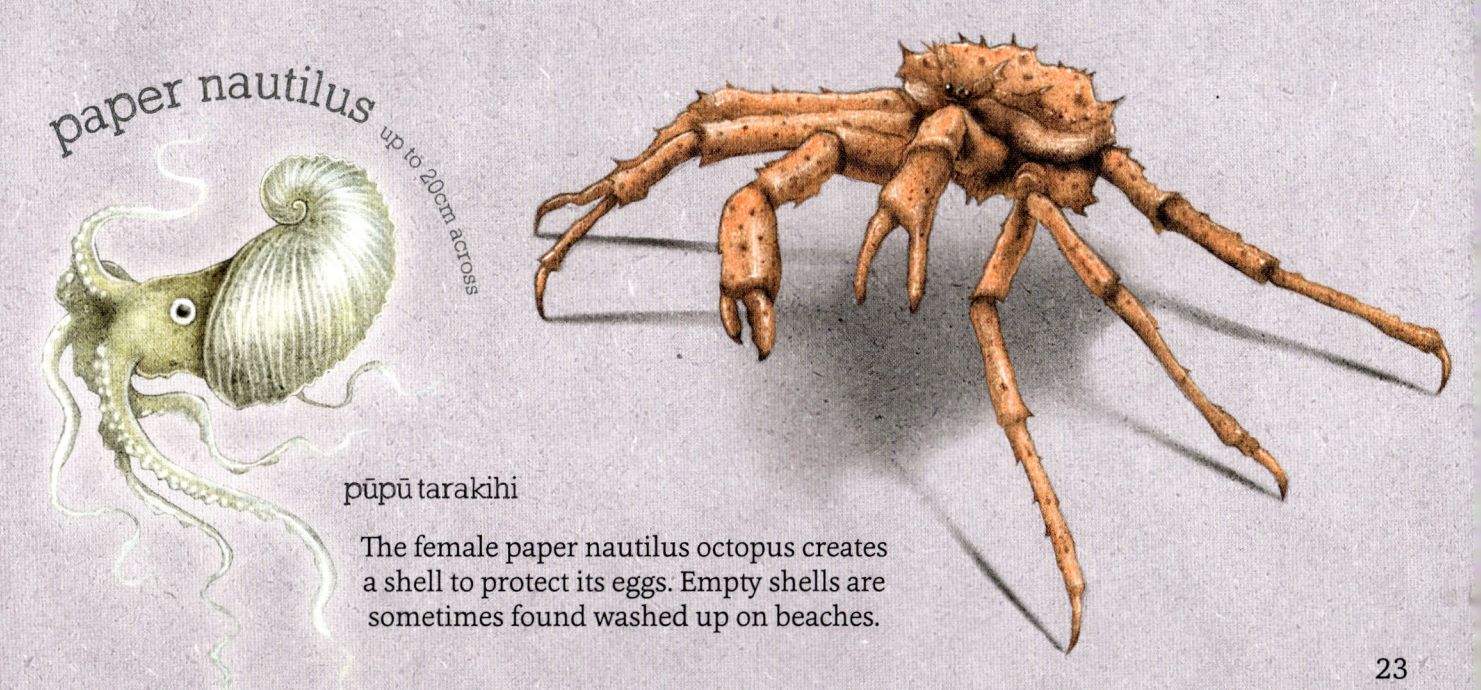

paper nautilus up to 20cm across

pūpū tarakihi

The female paper nautilus octopus creates a shell to protect its eggs. Empty shells are sometimes found washed up on beaches.

rays & sharks

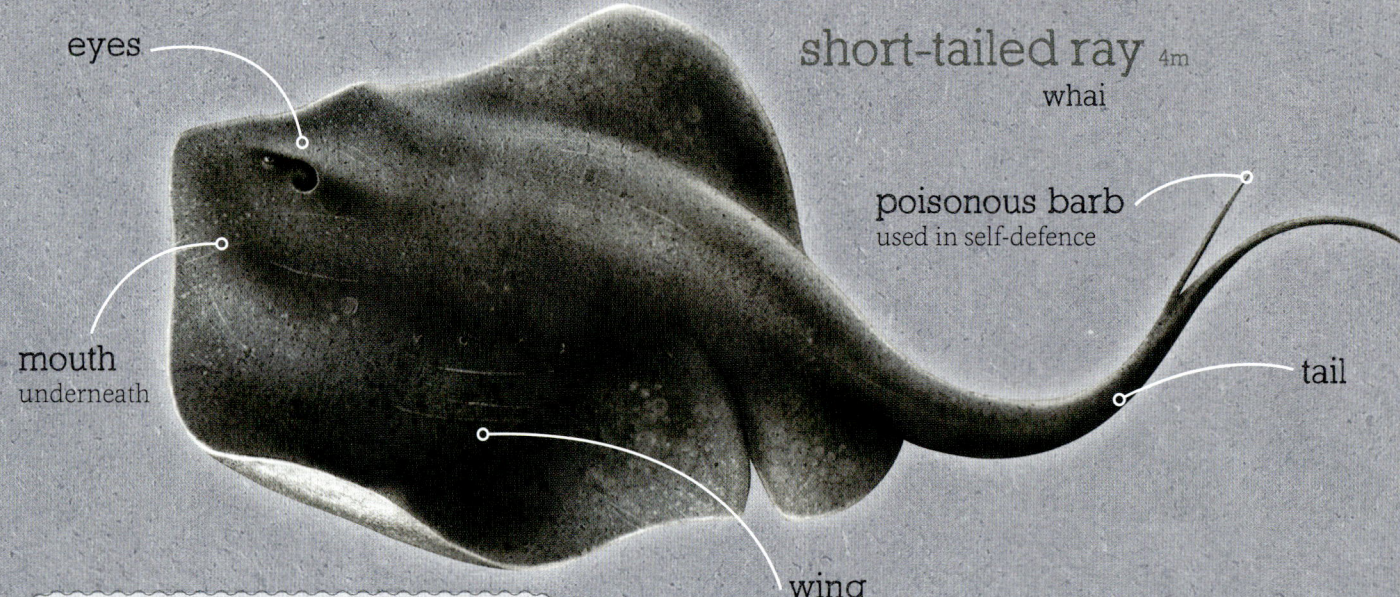

short-tailed ray 4m
whai

- eyes
- mouth — underneath
- poisonous barb — used in self-defence
- tail
- wing — used for swimming

ray facts

- Rays are closely related to sharks. Both rays and sharks are fish.
- Rays live in sandy and muddy areas as well as reefs. Their flat bodies help them hide on the ocean floor.
- Despite their poisonous barbs they are hunted and eaten by orca.

electric ray 1m
whai repo

carpet shark up to 1m
pekapeka

Electric rays hunt fish and crabs at night. They stun their prey using an electric shock that they can generate from glands in their heads.

24   Carpet sharks eat fish, shellfish, octopuses and squid.

mako

mako shark up to 4m

hammerhead shark
mangō-pare

The position of the eyes of a hammerhead shark give it 360-degree vision.

Mako sharks have several rows of teeth that are replaced every few months so that they are always sharp.

great white shark
up to 7m
mangō taniwha

Great white sharks, also called white sharks, eat large prey such as whales, other sharks and seals. They can travel long distances: scientists have tagged white sharks and tracked them from the Chatham Islands up to Tonga, over 3000km.

shark facts

- The largest fish are whale sharks –12m, and basking sharks – 9m. These very large sharks eat plankton rather than hunt large prey.
- Most sharks give birth to live babies, but small sharks, such as the carpet shark, lay eggs.
- Sharks have always been a valuable resource for Māori and other Pacific peoples, not only for their flesh but also for their teeth.
- Some shark species are endangered by fishing practices, such as shark finning, where sharks are caught just for their fins. While some people might think it a good thing to have fewer 'dangerous' animals in the seas around New Zealand, sharks are an important part of the ecosystem. They help to keep the population of other sea creatures in balance.

more fish

orange roughy 60cm

blue cod 65cm
pākirikiri

Orange roughy live in the deep ocean where their large eyes make it easier for them to see. If they aren't eaten by a whale or caught in a fishing net, they can live up to 130 years.

Blue cod eat shellfish, crabs and small fish. They can live up to 20 years. During this time they change from brown to blue, and some change from females into males!

marlin 4m

bill

Marlin feed near the surface of the ocean and can use their bill to stun or kill their prey.

fishing facts

- Overfishing – taking too many fish or other sea creatures – changes the balance of living things in the ocean. It can lead to a species becoming extinct and also affects other animals that rely on it for food.
- Some fishing methods can also kill other animals by mistake. Birds can get caught on fishhooks and sea lions and dolphins can get caught in nets.
- New Zealand has rules about how many fish and other sea creatures can be taken, as well as some marine reserves where fishing is banned.

moray eel 1.5m
kaingārā

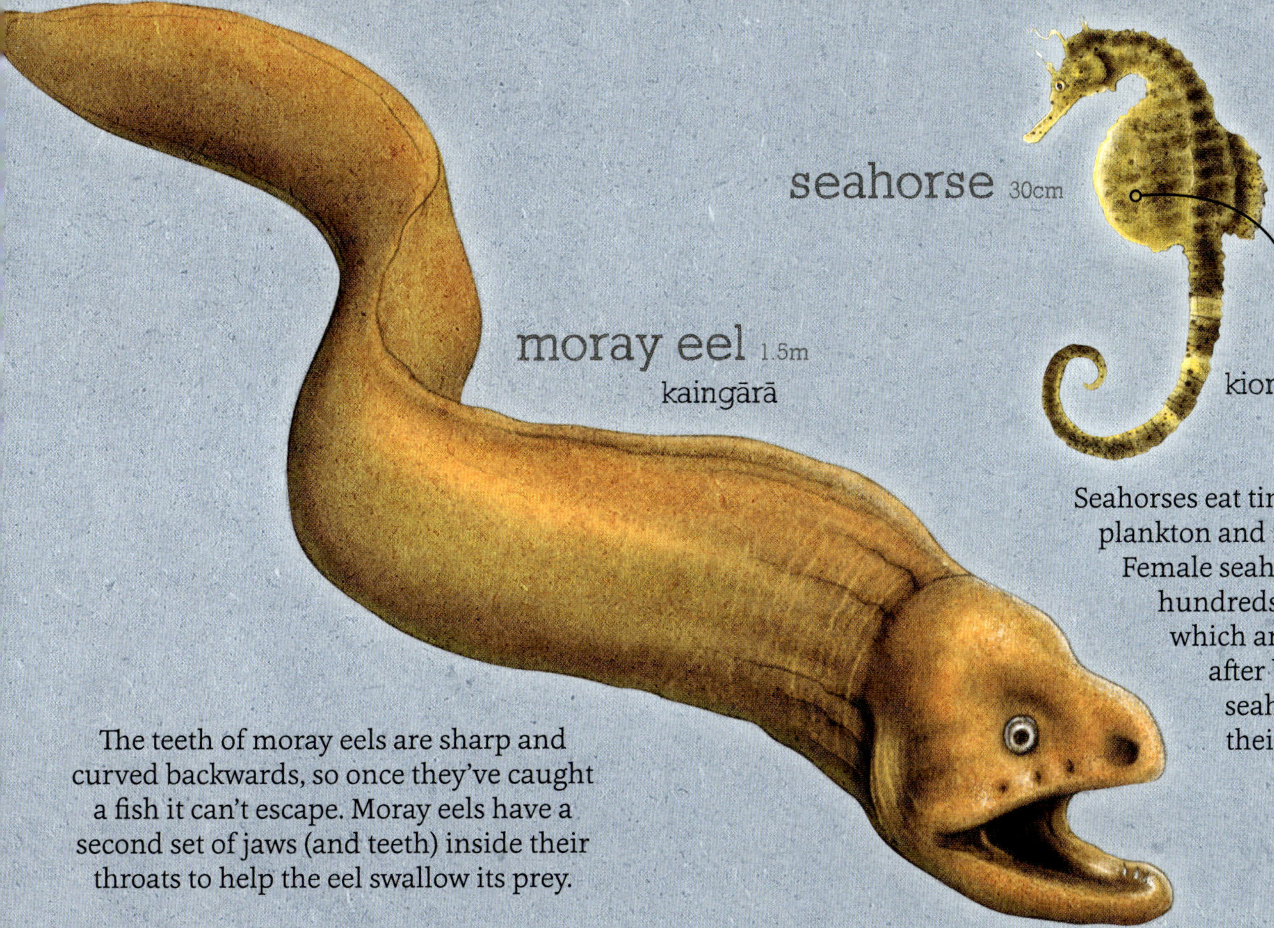

seahorse 30cm
pouch

kiore moana

Seahorses eat tiny animals, plankton and fish eggs. Female seahorses lay hundreds of eggs which are looked after by male seahorses in their pouches.

The teeth of moray eels are sharp and curved backwards, so once they've caught a fish it can't escape. Moray eels have a second set of jaws (and teeth) inside their throats to help the eel swallow its prey.

porcupine fish 60cm
kōpūtōtara

fish facts
- About 1400 different fish species can be found in New Zealand oceans.
- Fish start off life as eggs. Fish eggs and baby fish are in danger of being eaten by sea creatures and not many reach adulthood. Some, like the babies of seahorses or mako sharks, stay in the parent's body until they are larger and better able to survive.
- Scientists can tell the age of a fish by the number of growth rings on its ear bone.

Porcupine fish have strong jaws for cracking open shellfish, kina and crabs.

whales

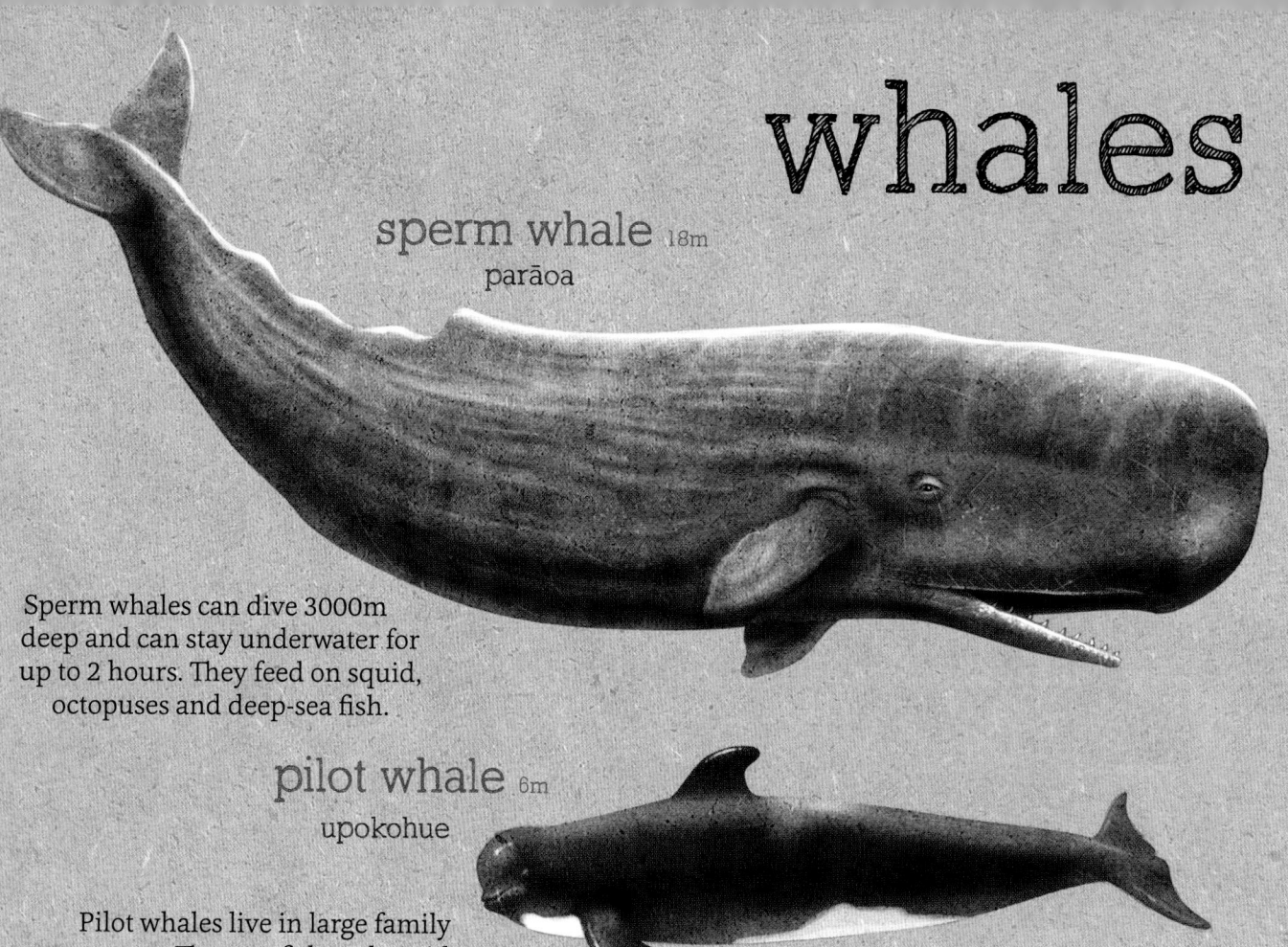

sperm whale 18m
parāoa

Sperm whales can dive 3000m deep and can stay underwater for up to 2 hours. They feed on squid, octopuses and deep-sea fish.

pilot whale 6m
upokohue

Pilot whales live in large family groups. They eat fish and squid and can dive up to 500m.

whale facts

- Whales need to come up to the surface to breathe, but unlike humans they can choose when to breathe.
- When whales breathe out you can see a 'blow'. This is from water that was around their blowhole along with moisture that was in their breath.
- Toothed whales, such as the sperm whale and pilot whale on this page, use echolocation to find prey. They make clicking noises and listen for any echoes. Echoes tell them that the sound wave has hit an object and been sent back in their direction. They can use this amazing ability to detect objects up to 800m away.
- Whales are sometimes found stranded on beaches. Scientists are still trying to figure out why this happens. Perhaps their echolocation is confused by sandbars.
- Many species of whale were almost hunted to extinction. Now most countries have agreed not to hunt whales anymore. Whales are still threatened by pollution and climate change which may lead to a loss of food that they rely on.

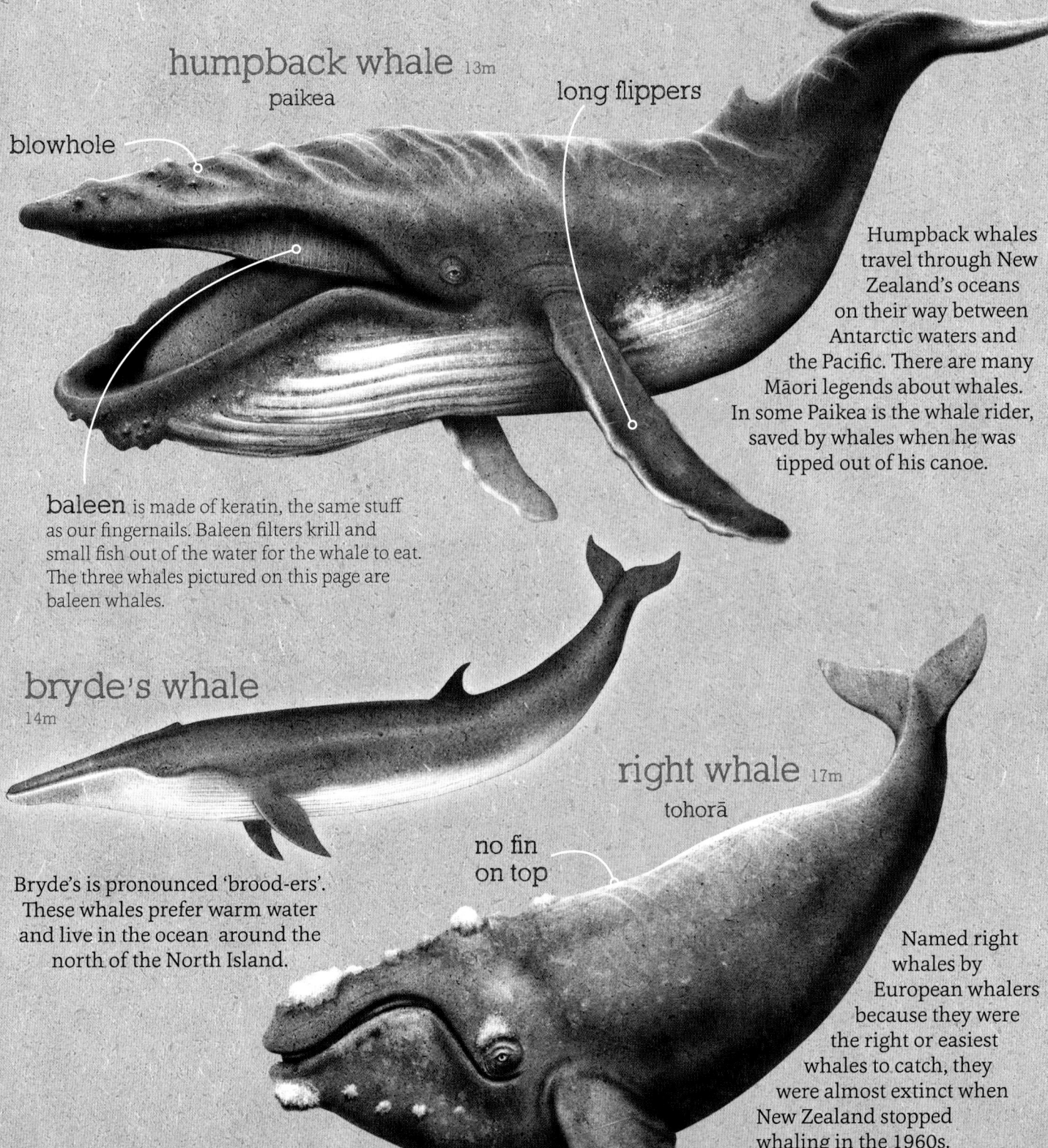

dolphins

dusky dolphin 2m

aihe

Dusky dolphins are well known for their acrobatics. They leap right out of the water.

bottlenose 3.5m

terehu

Bottlenose dolphins are seen in pods of up to 30. There are less than a thousand of them living around New Zealand.

common dolphin 2.6m

aihe

Both dusky and common dolphins sometimes come together in large schools of a thousand or more.

dorsal fin

orca 9m
maki

Some people call them killer whales, but orca are part of the dolphin family. Groups of orca come in close to shore hunting stingrays. They also hunt seals, small whales, dolphins, fish and squid. The male's dorsal fin can be up to 1.8m high. There are about 200 orca living around New Zealand's coast.

dolphin facts

- Dolphins eat fish and squid, which they hunt using echolocation.
- Dolphins communicate with each other using clicks and whistles, as well as through body movements such as leaping and tail slapping.
- While they often seem to enjoy swimming alongside boats they are sometimes cut by propellers. Fishing nets are also a threat to them, as a dolphin that gets stuck in a net will drown.
- Dolphins are very social animals and a few have become famous for their friendly behaviour towards humans, staying close to a particular beach and getting to know the locals. However, dolphins are still wild animals and people swimming near them need to remember this.

tūpoupou

hector's & maui's dolphins 1.5m

These small dolphins are only found in New Zealand's seas. It is easy to tell them apart from other dolphins, as they have a rounded dorsal fin and are much smaller. Hector's dolphins are found off the coast of the South Island, and Maui's off the North Island. Both live in shallow, coastal water which puts them at risk from boats and fishing activities. Maui's dolphins are the world's rarest and smallest dolphins and are a subspecies of Hector's dolphins.

seals & penguins

new zealand sea lion
females 2m, males 3m

whakahao

Also called Hooker's sea lions, they are the rarest seal species in the world.

fur seal
females 1.5m, males 2.5m

kekeno

Fur seals dive up to 200m deep for fish and squid. In the spring they gather on rocks in breeding colonies, where the mothers give birth to a single pup.

fur seal or sea lion?

- Take a look at the nose – if it's pointed then you've seen a fur seal, if it's blunt then it is a sea lion.
- If you saw it on a rocky shore it was a fur seal. Sea lions like sandy beaches but sometimes fur seals rest on sandy beaches too.
- Fur seals live all around New Zealand, while sea lions are usually only found in Otago and Southland. Most sea lions live around the Auckland and Campbell islands.

looking after seals & penguins

- It's best to keep a distance. Don't disturb them and they won't disturb you. Seals have sharp teeth and can move surprisingly fast on land.
- Help keep beaches and the sea clean. Seals and penguins can get tangled up in plastic and other waste.

yellow-eyed penguin 65cm
hoiho

Hoiho means 'noise shouter'. They might be noisy but they are also shy and prefer to nest away from other penguins in forests, flax and on farmland. The world's rarest penguin, it lives only around New Zealand.

little penguin
25cm

kororā

Also called little blue or blue penguins, they are the world's smallest penguins. They make nests in burrows or holes and will climb up to 300m to a nest site. Little penguins come ashore when it is dark, so you may have more chance of seeing one swimming in the sea during the daytime.

fiordland crested penguin 40cm
tawaki

These penguins can be seen around Westland, Fiordland and Stewart Island.

penguin facts

- There are more species living in New Zealand, if you include its offshore islands, than any other country in the world. The three on this page all nest on the mainland.
- Instead of using wings to fly in the air, the wings of these birds are more like flippers which help them dive and swim quickly. Their feathers keep them warm in the cold ocean.
- All penguins need to moult to replace their feathers once a year. This takes about a month and they can't swim (or feed) until their new feathers have grown.

seabirds

royal albatross
wingspan up to 3.5m

toroa ingoingo

These huge birds have the longest wings of any bird. Rather than flap their wings, they glide on air currents. This is an efficient use of energy and makes it easier for them to spend months out at sea flying huge distances across the ocean.

buller's mollymawk
wingspan up to 2m

toroa

Mollymawks are from the same family as albatrosses. Like other albatrosses, the Buller's mollymawk feeds on fish and squid at the surface.

fairy prion
length 25cm

tītī wainui

tubenose for removing salt from water

Fairy prions nest in burrows. On some islands, these burrows can be taken over by tuatara who will also eat any eggs or chicks that they find.

seabird facts

- Albatrosses, petrels, prions and shearwaters are all tubenose birds. Being able to get rid of the salt from seawater means that these birds don't need to return to land for fresh water.
- Seabirds, including penguins, catch fish and squid. They regurgitate this for their chicks to eat.
- Seabird colonies are smelly places. The birds' poo – guano – is rich in seafood and is good fertiliser for the land, as well as a source of food for insects.
- Threats to seabirds include fishing practices. They can get caught on fishhooks or tangled in nets.

sooty shearwater length 44cm
tītī

Also called muttonbirds, there are millions of sooty shearwaters. They breed in very large, closely packed colonies, mostly on small islands. Māori have traditionally collected tītī to eat and they continue to be an important food for some iwi.

westland petrel length 48cm
tāiko

Children from Barrytown School discovered the Westland petrel in 1945 when they were doing a school project. Westland petrels are at risk from predators such as rats and stoats.

gannet wingspan 1.8m
tākapu

Gannets can be seen flying above the sea spying for fish. Once they spot fish, they dive very fast – up to 145 kilometres an hour. Only about one-third of their dives are successful – if they don't catch a fish first go, they might stay underwater to chase fish, hoping for a second chance.

spotted shag height 70cm
kawau pāteketeke

Spotted shags dive from the surface and use their feet to help them swim underwater. Gannets and shags don't have nostrils, which makes it easier for them to dive. They breathe by opening their beaks when they are above the surface.

glossary

360-degree vision Ability to see all around itself without turning its head.
camouflage Colour or shape of an animal that matches an animal's surroundings so that it is hard to see.
colonies Large groups of animals or birds that live together.
crevice Narrow gap in rock.
currents Movement of sea water caused by powerful forces such as wind, tides and temperature changes.
echolocation Use of echoes to detect and locate prey. See Whale Facts page 28.
ecosystem Relationships and interactions between living things, and between living things and the environment they live in.
filter To take out tiny pieces of food from water or mud.

glands Part of an animal's body that can produce a chemical substance, or in the case of electric rays an electric shock.
migrate To travel somewhere to live, e.g. animals may migrate between a place they live in summer to the place they live in winter.
predator An animal that hunts and eats other animals.
prey Animals that are eaten by predators.
reef A ridge of rock and/or coral close to the surface of the sea.
school A group of fish.
species A group of animals (or plants) that not only look very similar but are capable of having young together.
tentacle A long flexible body part used for feeling, grasping or stinging.

index

anchovies 13
arrow squid 13, 14, 22
blue cod 11, 26
bottlenose dolphin 30
brittle star 10, 21
Bryde's whale 29
bryozoan *see* lace coral
Buller's mollymawk 34
carpet shark 11, 24
colossal squid 22
common dolphin 15, 30
crayfish 8, 23
dusky dolphin 30
electric ray 24
fairy prion 34
Fiordland crested penguin 33
fur seal 19, 32
gannet 35
giant squid 17, 22
great white shark 25
hammerhead shark 25
Hector's dolphin 31
hiwihiwi 10
humpback whale 29
kelp 10
king crab 23

kingfish 8, 13
krill 13, 20
lace coral 10, 21
little penguin 33
mako shark 14, 25, 27
marlin 26
Maui's dolphin 31
moray eel 27
New Zealand sea lion 32
nudibranch 9, 21
octopus 9, 23
orange roughy 26
orca 31
paper nautilus 23
pilot whale 28
plankton 13, 20
porcupine fish 9, 27
right whale 29
royal albatross 34
sea cucumber 11, 21
seahorse 8, 27
sea lion 19, 32
short-tailed ray 11, 24
sooty shearwater 13, 15, 35
sperm whale 17, 28
spotted shag 18, 35

stargazer 10
tarakihi 10
trevally 13, 15
tubeworm 7, 9, 21
tuna 13, 14
Westland petrel 35
yellow-eyed penguin 18, 33

find out more

Visit a marine reserve, check out books and DVDs from your local library or go to these websites:

www.kcc.org.nz Kiwi Conservation Club

www.teara.govt.nz Te Ara – The Encyclopaedia of New Zealand

www.doc.govt.nz/conservation/marine-and-coastal/ Department of Conservation

www.nzbirdsonline.org.nz New Zealand Birds Online

www.marinenz.org.nz Marine NZ information portal

Information for parents & teachers about this book:
www.craigpotton.co.nz/under-the-ocean